BACK TO
THE WOODS

BACK TO
THE WOODS

CYNTHIA CRUZ | POEMS

FOUR WAY BOOKS
TRIBECA

Library of Congress Cataloging-in-Publication Data
Names: Cruz, Cynthia, author.
Title: Back to the woods / Cynthia Cruz.
Identifiers: LCCN 2023004449 (print) | LCCN 2023004450 (ebook) | ISBN
    9781954245648 (trade paperback) | ISBN 9781954245655 (ebook)
Subjects: LCGFT: Poetry.
Classification: LCC PS3603.R893 B33 2023 (print) | LCC PS3603.R893
    (ebook) | DDC 811/.6--dc23/eng/20230202
LC record available at https://lccn.loc.gov/2023004449
LC ebook record available at https://lccn.loc.gov/2023004450

This book is manufactured in the United States of America and printed on
acid-free paper.

Four Way Books is a not-for-profit literary press. We are grateful for the assistance
we receive from individual donors, public arts agencies, and private foundations
including the NEA, NEA Cares, Literary Arts Emergency Fund, and the
New York State Council on the Arts, a state agency.

PROUD MEMBER

We are a proud member of the Community of Literary Magazines and Presses.

CONTENTS

Saint Paul, Virginia   3

Like We Were Never Born   5

Late Night Frequencies   7

Shine   10

Transmission   12

The Three Levels of Heaven   16

Riding   18

Father   20

All Night Home   22

Galax I   24

Mica   25

Small Wooden Music Box   27

The Overburden   29

Galax II   31

Vertigo   33

Mountains   34

The Temptation of St. Tony   36

After the Dream Came the Habit   37

Transmission   39

The Music   41

The Temptation of St. Tony   43

River Water   45

Dante, Virginia   47

Dark Register   48

Late Night Frequencies   50

A White Horse Walking Through a Field at Night   51

Alchemy   53

Born There   55

We shall not all sleep
But we shall all be changed,
It says in the Bible somewhere.

Blanket me sweet nurse
And keep me from burnin'
I must get back
To the woods dear girls
I must get back to the woods.

MARK LINKOUS

BACK TO
THE WOODS

Then, down at the Clinch
on my knees

gathering trace
of sediment
and the beautiful
poison of carbon.

This is where you walked
barefoot. Where you rode
the dry banks on motorbike
as a child.

Your mother, calling
and calling,
the dream crackling,

a long-distance phone call
arriving long distance
in a pay phone in a phone booth
in the lot of a Conoco
gas station.

The black tar of coke
burned by wire
rusting like tyranny
in the far-off field.

Prescience, the foreclosing.

A hand held in fire.

I woke alone
in a room
my mouth tasting of salt
of warm wet brine.

Where, I ask
is the fire boat,

the rustling pines
as you walk
backwards, out
from the lake
in your glimmering
white suit.

I met my mother when I was seven
in a river.

She was beautiful,
her long black hair
smelling of mountain.

Wurlitzer, and the broken
glass of black ice.

The shade of brush.

I was living then
among the hounds
and horses.

At night, I was listening
to intricate and more sinister
decibels.

The music of radio frequency.
The delicate scratch and crackle
that occurs between distant cities.

Black sediment and ash.

Old field recordings
begin their haunting.

One morning,
naked and flat
along my back
on a silver church pew.

There is no sky
and my hands
they are not mine.

In a stranger's suit
I wake
touching water,
deep inside
the warm dream
of another man's
disappearance.

LATE NIGHT FREQUENCIES

You are a car, you are
a hospital,

warm lights
at the edge

of a deathless
highway.

You are a truck
stop, a star.

You are water,
an engine

pulled out
from a car

and laid out
on a mountaintop

in a heatwave
in the middle of summer.

Compression, you are
death, benevolence

the blue of the moon
hovering over

the forest.
A child

fevered and loved
down to essence,

a silvery cream-
like substance.

Rabbits and endless
land.

A gun,
loaded.

You are a town
in the south,

abandoned.
You are sweet

coma,
the godly

swamp
of overdose.

A boy on silver
motorbike

racing through
the locked

wooden closets
of his childhood.

A girl,
in a yellow dress

walking through a field,
humming. You are

a strong god-like
substance

administered
by the nurse's
sweet hand.

If I had a home
it would be

a still in a film
where the sound
got jammed.

Me and my brother
when we were little

in the sun
with the beautiful
animals.

Old color photographs
Scotch-taped to the walls
of a farmhouse
in the Californias.

Dread, and its many
instruments of sorrow.

Did you love this world
and did this world
love you?

I don't know
the ending.

I don't know
anything.

I am dumb
and I am

simple and afraid
of everything.

But in winter
in the pines
is the wind

and the dissonance
of siskins

like Mellotron
flooding out

from its spiral
branches.

TRANSMISSION

This poem is a cassette
tape

the murmur
of your voice

recorded back
into the black

gauze of its matte
ribbons.

Its blur of tape
unspooled,

undone, then damaged
by hand.

Ruined by wire.
Its soft gauze

rubbed over
with muck

and layers
of ancient

dream-like junk,
wet with death.

The noise of truck
engines,

and the magnificent
fever of a boy

rifling through
the blue

and endless
woods

on his shining
motorbike.

Visceral and film-like
the gluey animal-

like substance drug
in from the trash.

Distortion
as magic.

Rupture as means
of making.

Sweet, the needle
as it tremors

between the static
of shortwave radio

stations. This song
is a failure,

a gun, a beautiful
woman,

nicotine-stained
fingers, trembling

on the hand
of a man.

A violin
played by an orphan

in a wooden chair
in a field

during an ice
storm.

Violence,
a stutter, a letter

constructed wholly
of quiet,

hum and fragment.
And crackle.

And silence.
Underwater

inebriation,
soft rupture.

Wordless, preverbal,
the sadness, broken,

distilled, and then
re-fractured.

I woke up in a burnt out basement
my body covered in slurry

my hands and face
coated in muck.

Marred with glitch

cracked and mangled
like satellites
crashing into a giant gas.

The static
of tape drop-out
cut with wow
and flutter.

If I had a home
it would be

constructed entirely
of animal

murmur and the blur
of Novatron.

Radio signal
mutilated by wire.

Then, smeared
over with Carolina.

A tiny cassette
with my own voice
as a child
inside the blur
and spell of fever.

The smell of dust
and the orange
sun's mottle at dusk.

Milkweed and thistle.

The smallest taste
of sleep

as spirit
enters

then
finally exits
the body.

I am better when I am dead
or when I am
sleeping.

Having finally entered
the carboned piston
of your machinery.

You, as a boy,
racing through
the warm excess
of night's soft decline.

When I rise
I kerosene
my fingers

place my hands flat
on its weeping
branches.

The music is smashed
Wurlitzer, trashed and drug
up from a landfill
in Tazewell.
Earth mixed with birth
and the bright peal
of a mangled glockenspiel.

In winter hills
of summer, sick,
the foal in the barn,

and an old farmhouse,
with all of its clocks
pulled out.

Its cold rooms
filling miraculously
with the slow
sediment of forget.

Zachariah is the name for sugar
can you tell him that
he said
walking out of the dream.

In Bible study
he said, *Cindy*
you are saved.

He poured milk into the tea
and gave me a belt
to ward off
the darkness.

I'd ride out with him
into the country
in his old station wagon.

And he'd point to the places
where God had been:

tiny near-invisible *x*s,
he said, counting
under his breath.

He'd been to the war
and ran for miles
every night
to race the violence
out of his body.

In the end, it's just a small
mark, the place
where the outside
tears in.

Stamps its human hand
on the spirit.

ALL NIGHT HOME

1

I saw an angel drop
into the small body
of a sick child.

I heard its warm white engines, and
I turned away.

2

She sits on the edge
of Manhattan Ave.
scratching the silver muck
off the small yellow, gold and red
cards with a silver coin
trying to find
its hidden number.

3

In a delirium
down the avenue.

4

Dinghy boat on river water.
Sunlight as chaser.

5

No matter what
I cannot make
the fixative

stop
this picture
from bleeding

its warp and gorgeous
instruments
back into me.

GALAX I

Trapped inside
your earthly body,

cut loose, finally
from the world.

Radiant, your face,
the face of a man

who has just barely
escaped his own death.

With what
voice

remains
inside the body

lead me back
to the room

where you are no longer
not human.

Already, we raced
through frequencies
of night

the woods unraveling
her wet metallics
back into us.

Diamond of light
and the inaudible
murmur of animals.

A humming
like the hour
when an unlucky
birth occurs.

Always, a mottled pony and hounds
milling in the dark yard.

The dead engines
of cars.

Always
your thin body
concealed

inside the sepulcher
of a white suit.

Your hands.

SMALL WOODEN MUSIC BOX

Exquisite, the violin song
cut from the twentieth century
Appalachian field recording.

Then spliced back
into the unseen

ruptures and gaps
inside this poem.

Filling this room.

Or, maybe
a radio playing

breaking static
and crackle

from the worn dash
of an old royal blue
Ford pick-up truck.

Parked in a car lot
near a field

in southern Virginia
during the last
hours of midnight.

The act or an instance
of getting free from.

The most delicate
ballad constructed
of nothing

but the hum
of your voice.

The smallest song
of how your life

could have been

and how not
to enter back
into it.

Through the gelatinous
and rotting gardens
of morning.

And indecipherable,
the nothingness of milk
and flowers.

When they found you
in that hotel room
you were still dreaming.

The window, a star
smeared with sorrow
like a jar of warmed,
white whiskey.

Outside, the abandoned bodies
of cars and silver
engines.

A charger in the yard
glimmering in the sun
like a tooth, held
underwater.

The sound of your voice,
a girl's, in a field recording
trapped on cheap plastic

microphone, set to the tune
of a far-off waltz.

Of violin and voices
recorded from bars and locked
stalls of filling station
bathrooms.

Leaning against a wall
of the ruins

struggling to wake
from the stupor

of the obscene
dream that is
America.

At night there were silent
parades of horses.

The sky was a black
spill of coke.

The wedding of darkness
and infinite
darkness.

The dream unfolds
from the bottom of the boat.

You lead me to the water
where the tide
smells of sulfur,

the brine of death
overtaking its edges.

There are starlings
in the branches

of pine trees and hiding
inside the blanks
of night.

Tiny white and yellow
flowers in the earth.

When I kneel down
to the wet ground

I hear the silence of engines
rusting in a far-off field.

The static of invisible
filaments trapped in air,

minerals
coming undone.

That night, like a soft door
opening.

By then
I had fallen in
with the beautiful
ranks of strangers.

The miracle of existing
within the small seconds
between dream and death.

I am entering
the rooms now

the doors opening
one by one—

And I can hear
the car radio
on the highway

and the silence
that is the absence
of God.

In the woods
below the snow

you were sleeping
inside the mines
for half a century.

In your white
store-bought suit
black work boots,
wild honey in your hair
and your face

made magnificent
from decades of dreaming
the same blurred dream.

The yellow lights
flickering, the blind
ponies dropping down
into the warm black
poison of slurry.

When they carry
our bodies,
will they carry
our bodies
by horseback or train
coach, riverboat or
by motorbike.

Will they drown us
at sea, set us back
into the cold
crib-like craft.

Then, will God
finally touch us
with his fingers,

let us go back
home, wade in the blue
sea of river,
together, again.

And the underworld police
in the underworld

playing chess, smoking
Estonian cigarettes

eating warm butter-
scotch pudding

and drinking
warm Cola

with the German
philosophers.

AFTER THE DREAM CAME THE HABIT

I woke last night
in a river.

How I got there
I don't remember.

It was the sound
of AM radio

the static that occurs
in the space between worlds.

Like turbulence or vertigo.
And in that blackness

I went searching
for my mother.

This is the problem
with the body.

It's like swallowing
a drug

or weather, or the mind
under duress.

You never know
what is going
to happen.

When God set me
here, upon this earth

already, it was
too late.

TRANSMISSION

I was back at the house
we had once been in.

Damage, and the smell of burned
ash and cheap bourbon,

fractured bits of plastic; a broken
accordion.

Old wooden floors, warped
and smelling

of birth
and gasoline.

Black sediment along the sills
and old rusted nails.

An empty glass.

Decades spent traveling
through one endless night.

Telephone calls made in cars
parked in car lots
of gas stations.

Or, driving
through a seamless
succession of days.

Or years. Nights in rooms
without location.

When I saw you last
your voice

was the voice
of a child.

Your hands, stained in the semblance
of darker elements.

Dear brother, let us
bury what we have left
in the earth.

And let the world
return itself
back to us.

Constellations of evening.

Sweet, the smell of fire,
and filth of pines.

What is the sound
of driving back
through black
magnetic fields of night.

Play the record back.

Unpack the accident
down to its haunting.

Its smaller rooms,
its trash and crackle.

This morning
the good voice
spoke to me.

A ghost
entering back
into the body.

Then the sound
of a mandolin playing.

What I was
is gone.

Now just the din
and smaller sounds

of wayward and crawl.

THE TEMPTATION OF ST. TONY

The devil was put here
to crawl upon this earth

someone once told me
the night before
I was born.

Rain, search lights,
and the sweet smell
of prison water.

Somewhere a room
is filling with a dream

of infinite ruin, and
yellowing music.

I wanted
to kill off
the darkness,

to stop
its incessant
singing.

But he loves me
too much.

When I told him
who I was

he changed
my name.

I left everything I owned
in a car I parked
at the edge:

father's broken
guitar, his black
leather boots,

and a small tin box
with the frequencies
of birth
crammed into it.

The smell of cherries
and cigarettes.

Water, a gun, and rabbits.

Yellow shimmer and the decadence
of near-death.

Disguised now
so they cannot
find me:

send their dogs and police cars
sirening after me.

I won't be dragged
back

by long black
stretcher like the girl
they found

hid in a swamp
surviving for weeks
inside the belly of a log.

Living for months
inside the oxide

shine, the damaged
and cracked

paper casing
of dreams.

The static of cotton
and wire.

Then the second
lesser kingdom began.

Dangering into another kind
of weather.

DANTE, VIRGINIA

Two pretty teenage girls
at the bottom of the hill
in bright red and yellow.

Pushing bills
into the shining
silver soda machine.

River, and delicate,
a hillside of mountain.

At night, a white horse
moving through

the collapsing
histories
of night.

If you leave,
he said,
keep who you are.

Don't let the world
and its desires
ruin you.

But after the dream
comes the habit.

And no way to fix it.

What is gone
cannot be put back.

Damage
from the inside.

What I have become
is warmed over

with that now
ancient dream.

What I was
is vanished.

I came back home
but I came back
gone.

A man stands
in the yard,

his hands
touch the warm metallic.

The smell of gasoline
and the hum that is night's
oscillating interior.

My hands, they touch
the hands of the man

his hands
touch the heat
of the engines.

A premonition, I covet
like a promise.

What instruments and where
shall we go

when, finally,

we abandon
our bodies.

A WHITE HORSE WALKING
THROUGH A FIELD AT NIGHT

The sweet voice
spoke to me again
this morning.

I was listening
at the window

for the patrol cars
along the river,

and the sky crackling
like wire.

Meanwhile, the infinite
armies have begun
to assemble.

The last time I saw you
your hands were bruised,
and your face

was marked
with the exhaustion
of sorrow.

Death was always
your friend
and you let it—

following its small
warm dream
down

into the small heaven
of the blackening fields.

When I was a child
father would take me
with him on the road.

We'd sit along the crimson
leather seats of the booths
in the quiet diners
of highway truck stops.

Eating nothing, drinking
waters and root beer.

His face was not his face.
It was the face of his father,
and his father's
father, years of labor
pressed, like a miracle,
into the shimmering oracle
of his dark countenance.

Warped and damaged
like a map
held underwater
for centuries.

We never spoke.

He was like a God to me.

The way he kept himself
inside himself

as if his spirit
belonged to him.

BORN THERE

I remember the ventilators
of childhood.

Its broken machineries,
its duct-taped engines
and shut windows.

Racing with my brother
after rattlesnakes and rabbits
down the dusty path.

Food stamps, lost maps,
slips of paper, and plans,
with names and numbers
of what I can never
remember.

Waking, on the cold tile floors
of hotel
bathrooms.

Once I was a girl

wading in a cream
dress into the lake.

This is not a parable
or a fairy tale.

If you had asked me then
what I wanted

I would have said
Nothing.

NOTES

"You are a car, you are a hospital" in the poem "Late Night
  Frequencies" is from the Sparklehorse song, "Saturday," from
  the album *Vivadixiesubmarinetransmissionplot.*
In the poem "Shine," "Did you love this world / and did this
  world / love you?" is from the Granddaddy song "He's Simple,
  He's Dumb, He's the Pilot" from the album *The Sophtware
  Slump.*
"I woke up in a burnt out basement" from the poem "The Three
  Levels of Heaven" is from the Sparklehorse song "Spirit
  Ditch" from the album *Vivadixiesubmarinetransmissionplot.*
  Reference to "satellites / crashing into a giant gas" is from an
  interview with Mark Linkous.
The poem title "All Night Home" is the title of a Sparklehorse
  song from the album *Good Morning Spider.*
In the poem "Vertigo," the lines, "By then / I had fallen in
  / with the beautiful / ranks of strangers" comes from the
  Sparklehorse song "More Yellow Birds," from the album *It's a
  Wonderful Life,* in which Linkous writes "I fell in with snakes
  in the poisoned ranks of strangers."
"Mountains" is a reference to the Sparklehorse song of the same
  name from the album *Dreamt for Light Years in the Belly of a
  Mountain.*
"The Temptation of St. Tony" references the Estonian film by
  Veiko Õunpuu of the same name.

In "River Water," "Water, a gun, and rabbits" is a reference to
Mark Linkous' line in his song "Saint Mary" from the album
Good Morning Spider. Linkous' reference is, itself, a reference
to the mythology of Frank Stanford's poetry.
"Born There" takes its title from the Frank Stanford poem of the
same name.

ACKNOWLEDGEMENTS

Academy of American Poets Poem-a-Day
The Colorado Review
Foundry
The Iowa Review
jubilant
Overbird Poetry
Plume Poetry
Poetry Magazine
Rainbow Agate
The Yale Review

ABOUT THE AUTHOR

CYNTHIA CRUZ is the author of seven collections of poems including *Hotel Oblivion,* which won the National Book Critics Circle Award and was a finalist for the Kingsley Tufts Award. She is also the author of *Disquieting: Essays on Silence,* a collection of essays exploring silence as a form of resistance, and *The Melancholia of Class: A Manifesto for the Working Class,* a book about Freudian melancholia and the working class. She is the recipient of fellowships from Yaddo, MacDowell and Princeton University's Hodder Fellowship. She lives in Berlin, Germany.

PUBLICATION OF THIS BOOK WAS MADE POSSIBLE
BY GRANTS AND DONATIONS. WE ARE ALSO GRATEFUL
TO THOSE INDIVIDUALS WHO PARTICIPATED IN
OUR BUILD A BOOK PROGRAM. THEY ARE:

Anonymous (14), Robert Abrams, Michael Ansara, Kathy
Aponick, Jean Ball, Sally Ball, Clayre Benzadon, Adrian
Blevins, Laurel Blossom, Adam Bohannon, Betsy Bonner,
Patricia Bottomley, Lee Briccetti, Joel Brouwer, Susan
Buttenwieser, Anthony Cappo, Paul and Brandy Carlson,
Dan Clarke, Mark Conway, Elinor Cramer, Kwame Dawes,
Michael Anna de Armas, John Del Peschio, Brian Komei
Dempster, Rosalynde Vas Dias, Patrick Donnelly, Lynn
Emanuel, Blas Falconer, Jennifer Franklin, John Gallaher,
Reginald Gibbons, Rebecca Kaiser Gibson, Dorothy Tapper
Goldman, Julia Guez, Naomi Guttman and Jonathan Mead,
Forrest Hamer, Luke Hankins, Yona Harvey, KT Herr, Karen
Hildebrand, Carlie Hoffman, Glenna Horton, Thomas and
Autumn Howard, Catherine Hoyser, Elizabeth Jackson,
Linda Susan Jackson, Jessica Jacobs and Nickole Brown, Lee
Jenkins, Elizabeth Kanell, Nancy Kassell, Maeve Kinkead,
Victoria Korth, Brett Lauer and Gretchen Scott, Howard
Levy, Owen Lewis and Susan Ennis, Margaree Little, Sara
London and Dean Albarelli, Tariq Luthun, Myra Malkin,
Louise Mathias, Victoria McCoy, Lupe Mendez, Michael
and Nancy Murphy, Kimberly Nunes, Susan Okie and Walter
Weiss, Cathy McArthur Palermo, Veronica Patterson, Jill
Pearlman, Marcia and Chris Pelletiere, Sam Perkins, Susan
Peters and Morgan Driscoll, Maya Pindyck, Megan Pinto,
Kevin Prufer, Martha Rhodes and Jean Brunel, Paula Rhodes,
Louise Riemer, Peter and Jill Schireson, Rob Schlegel, Yoana
Setzer, Soraya Shalforoosh, Mary Slechta, Diane Souvaine,
Barbara Spark, Catherine Stearns, Jacob Strautmann, Yerra

Sugarman, Arthur Sze and Carol Moldaw, Marjorie and Lew Tesser, Dorothy Thomas, Rushi Vyas, Martha Webster and Robert Fuentes, Rachel Weintraub and Allston James, Abby Wender and Rohan Weerasinghe, and Monica Youn.